Monster
Giggles

Written by Ken Ross
Illustrated by David Mostyn

HENDERSON
PUBLISHING PLC

©1995 HENDERSON PUBLISHING PLC

Why does every soccer team have a monster? Because they all have a ghoulkeeper.

Heard about the monster who soaked his top half in candle wax? He wanted to be wicked.

Why are monster babies less revolting than their parents? Because they are just a little ugly.

Why don't giants like polo? Because they prefer po-high.

YOU SAW A HEADLESS MONSTER IN THE GRAVEYARD?

YES, HONEST. AND IT WAS WEARING GLASSES.

There is no mistaking the Yeti.
It has dandruff as big as confetti.
It has huge teeth like spears
And blows fire from its ears
And is married to a Yeti called Betty.

The beast of beastly Beast Hall
Is pleased when pedestrians call.
He invites them to dine
And gives them strong wine
Before eating them skin, bone and all.

A monster with eleven feet went into a shoe shop and asked for five pairs of shoes.

The assistant gave him five pairs of shoes, then asked why he was leaving his eleventh foot uncovered.

THAT'S FOR TYING THE LACES

TUTOR: How do you know he was an alien?	STUDENT: He said he was from another univers-ity.

An earth-sucking monster from space
Sucked soil from his own planet's face.
He came here a hero
But sucked a volcano
And erupted all over the place.

There was a young monster called Fred,
Who always ate biscuits in bed.
His mother said, "Son,
That's really not done!
Why don't you eat humans instead?"

MONSTERS' MENU

Egg, chips and human beans

Shepherd's eyes

Steak and kids' knees pies

Beans on ghost

Cornishman pasty

Babies and mash

The living and onions

Fish and chaps

Tom's heart in soup

Stu and dumplings

Ma'am laid on toast

High scream cornets

Pineapple chumps

Please leave tips
(preferably whole fingers)
in the tray.

AAAAAAAAAAAAARGH

TOP TEN JOBS FOR MONSTERS

1. Traffic warden

2. Dentist

3. Dinner lady

HMM! YES! I THINK I'VE GOT A TUMMY ACHE!

4. Doctor

5. Grave digger

6. Head teacher

7. Great Aunt Elspeth

8. Prison officer

9. Caretaker

10. Librarian

There was a young monster from Harwich,
Who behaved very badly at her marriage.
She proceeded on skates
To the parish church gates,
While her groom followed on in the carriage.

There once was a monster from Leith
Who had most remarkable teeth;
They were ever so strong
And spiky, and long
And he kept each one wrapped in a sheath.

What do you give a monster with big feet?

Plenty of room.

What's the definition of a skeleton?

Bones with the people scraped off.

What do you call a witch who goes to the beach but won't go in the water?

A chicken sand-witch.

Where do you find monster snails?

On the end of monsters' fingers.

Why shouldn't you keep a two-headed monster?

Because it costs twice as much to feed.

A cannibal monster went on his holidays. When he returned, he had both legs and both arms missing...

... "What happened?" asked a concerned friend. "Oh nothing," said the cannibal monster, "it was a self-catering holiday."

Heard about the monster who ate lamp posts? He stood around on roadsides feeling light-headed.

Heard about Dracula's new boat? It's a blood vessel.

The tooth fairy left 20p under a baby vampire's pillow.

Mummy vampire complained over the stingy amount.

"If that's all the fangs I get, I won't bother next time," said the tooth fairy.

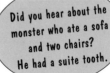

Did you hear about the monster who ate a sofa and two chairs? He had a suite tooth.

What do you call a monster who's black and blue all over? Bruce.

TWEET

What do you get if you cross a monster with a canary? A big yellow thing that goes 'tweet'.

MAN: Doctor, I've an insatiable appetite for corpses.
DOCTOR: Has anybody noticed?

What do you call a monster that's small and attractive? A failure.

MAN: I keep robbing graves.
DOCTOR: And what does Graves think about this?

What's big and ugly and has red spots?

A monster with measles.

What's big and ugly and bounces?

A monster on a pogo stick.

What's big and ugly and has wheels?

A monster on roller skates.

I wish you would stop frightening that boy.

Honest, I never spook to him!

... by B. A. Devil

WHAT MONSTERS DON'T LIKE ABOUT THE HUMAN WORLD:

CAMERAS - they snap back.

ZEBRA CROSSINGS - it is cruel walking on them.

SPOT CREAM - makes humans taste oily.

COMPUTER GAMES - show monsters as monstrous.

SLIPPERS - they are always too small.

NEEDLES - find them difficult to thread.

REMOTE CONTROLS FOR TVS - buttons too small.

FAST FOOD SHOPS - don't sell wildebeest.

CHRYSANTHEMUMS - can't pronounce it.

WRIST WATCH WEARERS - watch straps get stuck in teeth.

SKINNY HUMANS - need too many for a decent meal.

CHILDREN - who cry when being eaten.

RUBBER GLOVES - seem like fearsome creatures.

PINEAPPLE CHUNKS - tins hard to chew.

MONSTER MOVIES - not real monsters in starring roles.

DON'T WAKE THE GHOST ...

TRUE OR FALSE? The first monster ever to be captured by humans was known as The Seven Headed Serpent of Stratford.

During the reign of Queen Elizabeth I a reward of twenty-five pigs was offered to any citizen who could capture a living monster. Jonathon Snort, who lived two houses away from the great playwright William Shakespeare, is said to have trapped the beast in 1598. He dug a huge pit in a wood near Stratford-upon-Avon and waited by the pit for almost a month. One evening, when he was near to quitting his all-night vigil, a hideous cry came from the pit.

Jonathon Snort called locals to investigate and, when daylight fell, the people of Stratford-upon-Avon discovered a hideous serpent with, they claimed, seven heads.

YE UGH!

Later it was confirmed that the creature only had four heads, and its screams were a result of it having extremely bad teeth. Days later the monster died after a local man gave it a self-invented cure for toothache.

Jonathon Snort was made a lord, and when he died in 1613, he was buried next to the monster on a hill overlooking Stratford.

The awful truth? I don't think so. There are no hills in Stratford. Or are there...?

Why don't monsters get measles? Because they have no weak spots.

Why can't monsters ski? Because they are abominable snowmen.

"Here's a good book," said the sales assistant to Mrs Monster. "It's called How to Help your Husband get Ahead."

"Ooh no," said Mrs Monster, "he's got two heads already."

What did Dr. Frankenstein say when his monster couldn't do simple arithmetic? "You haven't got the brains you were born with".

Tarzan was swinging through the jungle one day, when he swung high above the canopy of trees into an evil cesspit of horror. He was surrounded by his worst nightmares - goblins, spooks, trolls, yetis - every hideous, evil-smelling creature you could imagine. Do you know what he said? "Oops, wrong joke..."

I don't know what to make of my husband these days.

How about a casserole?

Why do my friends call me a vampire?

Just eat your soup before it clots.

What's a vampire's favourite food?

Leeches and scream.

What are Dracula's girlfriend's favourite jewels? Tomb stones.

What has webbed feet and fangs?

Count Quackula.

Who is the best vampire maths teacher? Counter Dracula.

What's big, red and ugly?

What's scary and used for writing essays? A ballpoint monster.

An embarrassed monster.

What's big, red and has four wheels? A monster in a mini.

What do you get if you cross a fridge with an angry monster? A nasty cold.

What do you do if you find a monster in your bed? Sleep somewhere else.

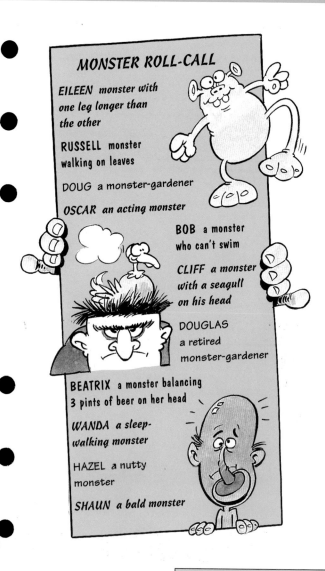

MONSTER ROLL-CALL

EILEEN *monster with one leg longer than the other*

RUSSELL *monster walking on leaves*

DOUG *a monster-gardener*

OSCAR *an acting monster*

BOB *a monster who can't swim*

CLIFF *a monster with a seagull on his head*

DOUGLAS *a retired monster-gardener*

BEATRIX *a monster balancing 3 pints of beer on her head*

WANDA *a sleep-walking monster*

HAZEL *a nutty monster*

SHAUN *a bald monster*

A great hairy monster from Datchet
Attempted to shave with a hatchet.
When his nose he did sever
He said "Now I'll never
Have nasal catarrh - I can't catch it."

A monster who lived in the Amazon
Tried to put nighties of his grandma's on.
The reason was that
He was far too fat
To be able to fit <u>his</u> pyjamas on.

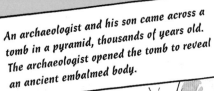

An archaeologist and his son came across a tomb in a pyramid, thousands of years old. The archaeologist opened the tomb to reveal an ancient embalmed body.

"What's that?" asked the son.
"A mummy," replied the archaeologist.
The son looked puzzled, "If that's a mummy, then where are her kids?"

... by Gibbs D. Jitters

A bright red monster named Rudolf was sitting at home gazing out of the window.
"I want to play golf, but rain's stopped any chance of that," he moaned.

His wife bustled in. "It's not even rain, I'm afraid, darling," she said.

"Yes it is!"   "No, it's not!"

"Yes, it is, Rudolf the Red knows rain, dear."

Monsters are reasonable house guests
Although neighbours may find them alarming
But if kept in bow ties and string vests
They often are looked on as 'charming'.

OH! HOW SWEET!

A vampire who needs to keep drinking
Sucks blood by the gallon upstairs.
A mummy that's rotten and stinking
You can hide under cushions and chairs.

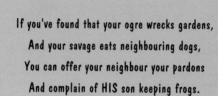

If you've found that your ogre wrecks gardens,
And your savage eats neighbouring dogs,
You can offer your neighbour your pardons
And complain of HIS son keeping frogs.

But if your wolf, ghoul, fiend or horror
Takes a dislike to those next to you
And devours them in night-times of terror
Well, there's nothing more you can do...

A ghost teacher was showing her pupils how to walk through walls. "Now did you understand that, class?" she asked. "Because if not, I'll go through it again."

How do monsters protest? They go on demonsterations.

Where do monsters go on holiday? Zombia.

Why do monsters have wavy hair? They drink sea water.

FRANK ANSWERS FROM MONSTER FRANK ANKLECHEW

Q: Is it true that monsters hate people?

A: No. Usually we just eat children. We don't care for old wrinkly skin.

Q: What do monsters do in their spare time?
A: Go ballroom dancing and dye their hair green.

Q: Where do monsters live?

A: In wardrobes, under beds, and especially in parents' bedrooms. Kids' beds are too small to sleep in.

... by Luke About

Q: Why do monsters frighten humans?
A: *If we didn't, we'd be on the dole.*

Q: Do monsters like jokes?
A: *Yes. Chomp!*
(remainder of questions asked without interviewer's head)

Q: When will monsters take over the world?
A: *About ten past seven.*

Q: Do monsters ever wear clothes?

A: *We wear batman costumes, and sometimes bowler hats.*

Q: Finally, what would you like to say to children?

A: *Put some salt & vinegar behind your ears, and maybe have a jar of salad cream ready. You'll taste better.*

SALAD CREAM

TOP TEN HUMAN MONSTERS

1. P.E. teachers
2. Strict parents
3. Nosy neighbours
4. Park keepers
5. School caretakers

6. Aunties with whiskers
7. Sweet shop owners
8. Brothers and sisters
9. Kids who have everything
10. Former best friends

The monster that swims in Loch Ness
Is often seen in a dress.
A reporter asked "why?"
The monster's reply:
"I wouldn't need to if I was photographed less".

A werewolf whose hair kept on growing
Put on clothes but the hair kept on showing.
Finally, in despair,
To lose all his hair
He laid on a lawn needing mowing.

Many years ago a huge shoal of plaice was swimming in an ocean near a tiny island. A mummy and a daddy plaice became separated from the shoal, and as they were finding their way back they discovered a baby monster struggling in the current.

The mummy and the daddy plaice rescued the monster. They took him back to the shoal, and there he lived happily for twenty-five years. Then one day he suddenly realised he was different. He went to his adoptive parents and asked them why he wasn't flat and silvery like they were. Why, after all this time, hadn't they told him the truth?

Mummy looked at daddy, then she looked at the monster.
"Son," she said softly, "we didn't want you to feel out of place."